At Grattan Road

GERARD HANBERRY

Best wishes,
Gerard Hanberry

salmonpoetry

Published in 2009 by
Salmon Poetry
Cliffs of Moher, County Clare, Ireland
Website: www.salmonpoetry.com
Email: info@salmonpoetry.com

Copyright © Gerard Hanberry 2009

ISBN 978-1-907056-06-2

All rights reserved. No part of this publication may be reproduced or transmitted in any form or by any means, electronic or mechanical, including photography, recording, or any information storage or retrieval system, without permission in writing from the publisher. The book is sold subject to the condition that it shall not, by way of trade or otherwise, be lent, resold or otherwise circulated without the publisher's prior consent in any form of binding or cover other than that in which it is published and without a similar condition, including this condition, being imposed on the subsequent purchaser.

Cover photography: Jessie Lendennie
Cover design & typesetting: Siobhán Hutson

The publisher and author gratefully acknowledge the financial support of Galway City Council toward the publication of this book.

Acknowledgments

Acknowledgements are due to the editors of the following, in which some of these poems first appeared, a number of them in slightly different versions:

Poetry Ireland Review, *The Stinging Fly*, *The SHOp*, *Trespass* (London), *Revival*, *Cyphers*, *Tintean* (Australia), *ROPES*, *Crannóg*, *Measure* (USA), *West 47* Online, *www.laurahird.com*.

Contents

I

Speech, After Dinner	13
Francis Bacon at The Tate	14
Your Day Ends at 2 p.m.	16
The Taste of Apples	17
Visiting France	18
The Final, Galway V. Kerry	20
User	21
Samhain	22
Reservoir	23
Outside of Town	25
Old School Tie	27
Heresy	28
February Skyline	29
Daybreak	30
Dawning	31
Craven Cottage, Saturday Afternoon	32

II

Hosting	37
Day of Reckoning	40
Continent	41
Forewarnings	42
Jack Frost	43
Manhood	44
The Earth Circles the Sun	45
The Great Empire's Heart	47
Trap	48
Liberation Day	49

III

By Kingston Bridge	53
The Scene	54
Tight Squeeze	56
Runaways	58
Don't Wait	59
Thameslink, Travelling South	60
Mystery	62
Dublin, Early Autumn	63
In Cannizaro Park	64
Credo	66
An Easy Way With Words	67
Lifers	68
Dead Windows	69
Circling, Circling	70
Folksong for Kitty	71
Company	72
Blink	73
Country Matters	74
Eyes of Blue	75
Cultural Evening	76
Gothic	77
Homecoming	78
Making Plans	79
Now That You Are Gone	80
The Reading	81

IV

Winner	85
Creatures of the Mist	86
Fatal Distractions	87
Meet the Punctuations	88
Ode to a Rejected Cliché	90
Sensing the Verse	91
The Way with Strangers	92
Trespasser	95

V

Old Vixen	99
The Lie	100
November	101
Nightwatch	102
A February Burial	103
The Day After	104
At Grattan Road	105
The Door	106
Barbs	107
Beggars	108
Birthday Drive	109
Intruder	112
Sorrow	113
Alone	114
No Gardener	115
Rituals: A Diptych	116
Solace	117
Wake Talk	118
Seeker's Lullaby	119

I

More and more I've learned to respect the power of the phrase, 'the greedy soul'. We all understand what is hinted at with that phrase.

>ROBERT BLY
>from *Intuitions and Ideas*, an essay published in *The Insanity of Empire*

And down the long and silent street,
The dawn, with silver-sandalled feet,
Crept like a frightened girl.

>OSCAR WILDE
>from *The Harlot's House*

Speech, After Dinner

So, gentlemen, I thought I'd mention
before finishing,
Diogenes the Cynic who lived in a barrel,
all trappings discarded,
only a loincloth and his drinking bowl –

when he saw a shepherd boy drink
from the river with his bare hands
that was the end of the bowl.

As for the loincloth –
found pleasuring himself in the marketplace
his unruffled comment was
he wished the hunger of his belly
could be so easily reduced.

No holy ascetic our Diogenes,
just a man with a certain take on the superfluous.

The Great Alexander once asked him what he wanted –
For you to move, replied the relaxing Cynic,
you're blocking my sun.

The Greek word cynic means 'like a dog'.
So thank you for having me
and I'll leave you Corporate Warriors
with that image –
the man with the bite in his bark.

Francis Bacon at The Tate

We fixed a price with the cab driver
who told us on the way down
that he was really a chemical engineer,

laid off last year
and now, at fifty eight,
had little hope of another job.

Even so, he continues to apply,
sending out CVs and checking the internet
every day, but no luck.

Driving puts bread on the table
but he is selling himself short,
don't you know, and it is dangerous work –

only last week a colleague was attacked,
robbed, his head opened, blood everywhere
and now they are using knives,

slitting cabbies' throats,
leaning in from behind your back,
they would rip you open, just like that,

and he clicked his fingers.
What's the world coming to?
No more night work, too bloody risky,

then you've got the drunks and druggies,
know what I mean, puking or defecating,
yes Sir, defecating right there in the back seat,

then you're off the road for a day
trying to clean up the mess and the smell,
and they don't give a toss,

enough to make you scream your head off,
sit behind the wheel in this tin box and scream
but what's the point, nobody's listening,

so you just keep going, know what I mean,
keep sending out the CV's, hoping for the best,
at least we're above ground…

We crossed the river at Chelsea Bridge,
swung into Grosvenor Road,
straight on to Millbank

then eased up to the Gallery's elegant steps,
Francis Bacon and his bestial distortions
already eyeing us from the poster beside the door.

Your Day Ends at 2 p.m.

(A notice in a hotel-room in Mexico City –
   from Truman Capote's *In Cold Blood)*

Someone from housekeeping, hopefully somebody kind,
cleared the last of your junk
into a black plastic bag.

Your few valuables had already disappeared.
Then a squirt of air-freshener,
who would ever guess?

Later, night-laughter out in the narrow hall,
a man, a woman in a red dress,
their drunken fumble with keys.

Lovecries and the headboard slapping
off the floral-patterned wall. The one we could hear
you climbing every night since you arrived.

The Taste of Apples

In the end it was the orchard drew him back
the villagers believe,
he missed the taste of ripe apples
plucked straight from off the branch.

The walled garden is being restored,
its tangle of brambles slashed, ivy hacked away.
They can see him working there on his own,
shirtless in the sun, bareheaded in the rain.

As a child he was jealous of the trees,
all the time they spent down there together,
just the two of them, pruning, fretting over disease
while he watched from the landing window.

Then years spent hiding out somewhere north,
living in the woods,
burning charcoal,
wild as a boar.

Visiting France

From our window table we can see the town of Sète
twinkling as night comes down. The toast
is to 'old friends and true'. The past and the future
off exploring their respective poles and may be some time.
The waiter looks proud of his recommendations.

A nearby eatery fires laser beams into the darkness.
Three electric-blue shafts swing hither and thither
through the skies of southern France like some futuristic blitz.
My quip about attracting a more celestial clientele
gets lost in translation so I sit there like a grown up,

all the while trying not to let on that a small saucer-like craft
has just landed in the car-park, a ladder has been lowered
and what must be a family of exhausted space travellers
is being led towards our door by a strange life-form
I take to be the father, followed by three smaller

yet identical creatures, each with the same shell-like back
and webbed feet. Taking up the rear is another adult,
probably Mom, her three bulbous eyes swivelling nervously
at the end of slender antennae, four pincer arms
outstretched, keeping her brood in line.

Once inside, I hear Mom remind her family
that it is rude to stare at the strange humans,
even though two of them are gouging soft white meat
from the shells of red crustaceans,
obviously alarming the new arrivals.

The visitors are shown to a nearby table
where their strange yet sad eyes become drawn
to the fish-tank in the corner and the crabs
and lobsters crawling about,
their claws restrained by rubber bands,

something the exiles, relaxing a little
after a good meal and a bottle or two of house red,
will later explain, filled them initially with dread
and a longing for their beautiful
but turbulent homeland many light years away.

The Final, Galway V. Kerry

(All Ireland Football Final, Croke Park, Dublin, 1964)

September sunshine, three o'clock,
the last Sunday of the month
and the great stadium
tense as the centre of an atom.

Irishmen in frenzies of isolation
shin up electricity poles
in Camden Town and Cricklewood
with coat-hanger aerials and battery radios,

wild attempts to snatch the faint transmission
from the city's begrudging air.
Later, around tables swamped with beer,
they will talk excitedly of old Connemara men,

dead this fifty years but up tonight
from their brambled graves and sitting
on granite rocks at the gable end
of roofcaved cottages,

anxiously watching the bothereen,
waiting for someone,
a traveller maybe or a youth with a car,
to bring them the wonderful news.

User

Skulking in his seedy peep-show life,
vaguely smelling of disinfectant,

enjoying the bare-naked vulnerability
of those on the floors below.

Feeling wanted only on the seamy side,
behind dark glasses and a ridiculous nose,

ignoring the blank expressions under the plastic smiles
beside him on his midnight pillow,

knowing this is as good as it's ever going to get
having had so little to invest.

Fearing the attendant might come hammering
at any moment on his booth's flimsy door,

and in the end, a life spent watching for hair
to grow bushy on the palms of his fetid hands.

Samhain

Firecrackers explode across suburbia
where youths stamp and jostle

in bristling packs
around chippers and video-stores.

The old sit in darkness, doors locked and bolted,
their TVs off, while taxis do a roaring trade,

back and forth from town or the off-licence.
The moon lurks, pucka-faced, behind flimsy clouds.

A coven of shrieking kids in glowing scream-masks
head for home with their trick-or-treat loot.

Firemen pray for rain. A blue Toyota, probably stolen,
roars across the tarmac at Early 'n Late, spins a doughnut

and is gone. A youth in a grey hoodie, his mobile glowing,
keeps watch from across the road

where the line of bare ash stand lance-long,
their last few leaves blowing about like funny-money

while out on the murky green, a piled bonfire sits
waiting for the sparks to fly.

Reservoir

> *Tell me about despair, yours, and I will tell you mine.*
> from *Wild Geese* by Mary Oliver

They built a cathedral near the river
where the old County Jail once stood
groaning in its own hanglong shadows.
Raised it up to high heavens
with chunks of limestone, hauled down
from Anglingham and Menlo, squared and dressed,
and a lead-green dome to cap it all off –
a job well done. Well done!

A Cardinal flew in from Boston for the grand opening,
a Prince of the Church no less. The townsfolk
stood around in their Sunday best, shaking hands
and slapping each other on the back while their kids
lined the pavements, waving yellow Papal flags,
bewildered but happy because their parents seemed happy,
and sheets of white sunlight rolled down the great stone walls
and bounced across the tumbling waters of the river.

My father left his pay-packet on the dresser,
looked at my mother and wondered what next –
there would probably be a few more weeks in it
tending to the snags when all the fuss died down –
then he drew a chair to the kitchen table
where the teapot sat on a cracked diamond of polished marble,
a damaged Italian tile from a side chapel, smuggled home
the year before in his coarse-canvas lunch bag.

There was probably a big dinner somewhere afterwards
for the Prince and the Bishop
and the men who came to work in suits, but my father,
because it was a perfect day for the job, came straight home

to boil up tar in the rusty half-barrel he kept out back.
(I can still remember the sticky-sweet smell of the black
liquorice as it bubbled in the cauldron and the thick smoke
curling around the house like a huge furry tail).

All week the downpour had been seeping through,
this time at the chimney,
oozing in waves down the wall by the fireplace
then in steady drips over by the shelves.
I'll tar and patch it the next fine day; a flat roof's no good.
Mother, sharp now from the throb of her despair,
wrings a towel – *It's a waste of time patching, patching,
and wasn't it yourself put on that flat felt-roof?'*

Knowing well her next line –
Why, in God's name, did I ever agree to come back here? –
I bit my lower lip and prayed a child's prayer
that my smarting father would not take the bait,
then watched from a corner of that little kitchen
as the dark ceiling-stain grew ever larger –
Iceland, Australia – a continent of fear,
a whole lifelong reservoir of it.

Outside of Town

I live outside of town
on the edge of a forest

the very rim of a continent.

No one calls, ever.
It's better that way.

My wife took off for London years ago
with a man she met in the village.

He was not from around here.

Times I hear voices upstairs, whispers,
a woman sobbing, a man comforting.

But I live alone, you see,
alone except for the rats

in the attic or down
beneath the floorboards.

I think they can get into the room
where I keep the newspaper cuttings

and the knives.

I go out only to buy food or petrol
for the old Volvo.

There's a girl with black hair on the checkout.

I pray but God never listens. Has God got ears?
Has He skin? Can He see me when there is no moon?

I ask Him for help but no help comes,
only silence or the wind through the rotting ash.

Sometimes I go into the room.

I like black hair.

Sometimes I go out after dark.

Old School Tie

Because in the old school yard
he was the Pied Piper who led the parade,
you let him in when he shows at your door.

He's been living the ascetic life on an island,
or so he says, in a hermit's beehive cell no less,
adding a mystical dimension to the yarn.

He describes in great detail the domed stone roof,
his bed of dried ferns and his friends the speckled
spiders, the ones with the frail legs like a giant M.

But you know him well enough. More likely he's been
hiding out in the woods where the Night Link turns,
living on cans and cold chips from Salt 'n Pepper.

You ignore the irony tinkling in his words of admiration
for the apartment and the way he runs his hand
along the polished granite countertop, as if to imply

it's far from this you were reared. He's no longer young
and should have moved beyond the same few chords.
Soon he will want something. First a book, to soften you,

then money which you will give him while vowing that
next time, he will be directed to the large tattooed sax player
busking every night outside the health food shop.

You will mention how his hat is always full, mostly
paper money, let slip that he has a wooden leg
and is, in actual fact, totally blind.

Heresy

If rambling through the many mansions of the hereafter
was all that it was cracked up to be,
what, I wanted to ask, had Lazarus to say,
hauled back, as he was, to live again
in a cruel land of dust and turmoil
with an army of occupation clanging about.

But rocking the boat was not the preferred option
back then with the smoky whiff of Inquisition
about the place, as the priest in his black cassock
swished up and down between the desks
and the town went about its own business
somewhere outside the walls.

We oozed from day to grey day
thinking about the Majors box stashed
behind the cistern, disowned if discovered,
and the glories of that solitary girly magazine
passed from hand to sweaty hand
and waiting that wet week, upstairs

between mattress and rusty springs,
patient as a wildcat all day in its dry lair,
listening for the scuffle of footsteps,
the probing fingertips,
throbbing in its fleshy sinfulness
for the silence of night to fall.

February Skyline

(Connemara, 2007)

Spring sunlight and Derryclare
bare shouldered in her silver gown,

low-slung, daring, best foot forward.
And look! The other peaks now join the drama,

majestic above their proud Barony,
stepping from cloud-shadow,

celebrating,
having wept their winter's fill.

Daybreak

If there is sound it is the low moan of sea-wind
through the bleached bones of lovers
chained high on the chalky face of the moon.

Dreams are rotting hulks doldrumed
in misty Sargasso thought-tangles.
When the sun appears it is a scarlet sky-dancer

loosing the night's black veils, and the bay
becomes a silver dish of severed fish-heads
spread between the blue hills and the islands.

Dawning

A stray dream-dog,
squat, broad-chested,
an ugly brute,
is limping through the tip-head
where toothless hags of nightmare
and some of their worst cronies
are hunkered down,
bony arms working through
the stinking mush.

One is wearing a red-laced bootie
(her other leg has sunk into the grey porridge)
something which vaguely
connects with a taxi ride, yes,
and the match of it glimpsed now
on the floorboards
where the dawn
is pooling close to
the foot of the bed.

Craven Cottage, Saturday Afternoon

Ex nihilo nihil fit.

The downcast crowd slumps up through Bishops Park,
the tide is out, the river low,
the evening closes in on Putney Bridge
with sheets of freezing sleet and squawking gulls.

A bus, and then another.
Blank faces at the windows stare ahead
at nothing, sealed inside their lives.
Three, nil…'nothing can come of nothing'.

— *Cheer up Pat! It can't get any worse.*
— *It will, it will. Fulham's for the drop, that's sure.*

The pub is packed with men yet feels subdued.
Pints of Young's bitter and whisky punch
to chase away the January blues,
and yet this gloom won't budge.

*We're all goin' down,
not just those fat-cat ponces on the pitch!*

Down…'down the iron stair we tramped',
each to his lot:

a bully on a Monday morning shift,
a wife who says she's fallen out of love,
a burning in the gut that's paid no heed,
a partner swapped, yet life remains the same,
we dreamed of something better once, but what?

– *Drink up lads!*
– *And don't forget the Cup game Wednesday night.*
– *I've told the wife her promise is on hold!*
– *Oh yea! Some chance mate, she'd have your fucking life.*
– *I'd love to win, just once, at anything.*
– *Before we all grow fat and bald and old.*

II

Last night we argued about the Marines invading Guatemala in 1947,
The United Fruit Company had one water spigot for 200 families,
And the ideals of America, our freedom to criticize,
The slave systems of Rome and Greece, and no one agreed.

        ROBERT BLY
        from *Sleet Storm on the Merritt Parkway*

Hosting

No fife and drum prancing,
no dispirited line trudging through fields of mud.
I see fresh-faced boys and some girls,

white, black, from Alabama maybe or the Mid-West,
wandering through an airport lounge
wearing sand-camouflage fatigues and light desert boots,

a little bewildered – *Shannon? Ireland?* –
all spit and polish respect in groups of three or four,
some queuing for the pay-phone,

others buddy-buddy around the drinks dispenser,
for all the world like well organised athletes
heading off to the Olympics

and not an army hosting
on their way to the Tigris and to war.
It looks almost normal, almost acceptable…

until I notice, in bar and bathroom mirrors,
their reflections, quivering like jet-fuel mist.
I see the businessman with a briefcase

making his way towards the gates,
a good suit slung in a black plastic zip-bag
– and I am reminded of death.

    ★

And of Xerxes, the Persian King marching on Athens
with the greatest army the world had ever seen.

When he arrived in Abydos, the people there had prepared
a throne of white carved marble set on a rise above the sea.

King Xerxes took his seat and looked down over the shore.
He saw the whole Hellespont hidden by his ships

and all the beaches and wide plains of Abydos filled with men.
Herodotus records – *he congratulated himself* –

and the moment after burst into tears.
It took seven days and nights for the army

of the mighty Persian empire to cross into Europe.
For all of that, he failed.

   ★

And what of those who return from such campaigns,
Assyrian and Caspian warriors,
Vanzant of the 2nd Infantry Division,
Jackson of the Stryker Brigade Combat Team.

Back home, their worlds reduced to night-vision green
even in broad daylight and lovemaking recalls
the jerky twitching of that young woman's body
lacerated with shrapnel in Mosul's market square.

My country's eyes averted
like a schoolgirl's from a pervert's flaunting,
as torture-planes and troop-carriers
land, fuel, rest, take off from our little riverbank airport.

   ★

Before Xerxes began his march against the Athenians
he set up provision dumps at carefully chosen sites along

the route. Nations were ordered to prepare entertainment
for him against his coming. Pythius, a wealthy Lydian,

offered his vast fortune to the King. The offer was refused
but the Lydian was handsomely rewarded for his generosity.

Later, emboldened by the gifts, Pythius came to Xerxes.
Would the Great King release one of his five sons

serving in his army in order to take care of his ageing
father and the estates? This was a mistake.

In a rage, the Persian King gave orders to find Pythius' eldest
son and cut him in half. The army then continued on its way,

advancing between the two halves of the young man's body,
one on the right hand side, the other on the left.

⋆

I drink a beer at the airport bar
and watch a father amuse his toddlers
with shoulder-highs and a colouring book.
The troops melt away through Departures.

Flights are called, people's names,
places we once heard only in classrooms,
in a sing-song voice, dates of battles,
capital cities, rivers of the world –

Boyne,
Shannon,
Tigris,
Euphrates,
Mekong …

Day of Reckoning

Today my mind is filled with
shiny thoughts, serrated,
slit-sharp on both sides.

Some are long-handled like Wexford pikes,
pointed and barbed, others short but lethal
as Assyrian daggers.

Today my heart is a coat of mail,
Persian mail, like the scales of a fish
made from the best silver.

When I speak,
my words will be steel-tipped javelins
fire-hardened.

I have glimpsed the enemy at last,
wearing fox-skin as headdress,
brightly coloured tunics to hide their sabres.

The oracles have been consulted.
Today my blades will not rest in their scabbards,
today my blades will draw blood.

Continent

On its knees, a great rhinoceros kneeling,
square chin propped on the cooked earth,

its huge body, wrinkled and leathery,
a grey sack full of dry sand.

Eyes definitely female, wide open, watching
two men in uniforms, one black, one white,

lob plastic rings onto her curved horn.
They are laughing, enjoying their game.

Nearby, three young boys in football shorts,
are playing on an ancient tractor,

tyres perished, engine seized,
abandoned, no rains to rust it away.

All about, the dusty vastness shimmers as if
seen through fuel-mist from a jet engine.

Beyond only silence, except for a faint humming,
imperceptible at first, but growing.

It's like the sound of countless insects,
trapped and seething in a huge glass jar.

Forewarnings

But oh, to be slipping ever backwards in time, the savage memories, the withheld cry!
   from *Owl* by C. K. Williams.

Take note, there were forewarnings,
the moon sweaty and swelling with desire,

she-men, bearded ladies,
that lamb born with the head of a child.

Creatures stalk the red desert,
out there with the reptiles and the hawks,

satellites have picked them out.
The next Pope will be black, it is said.

There's a tyrant swinging by the neck
in a Persian dungeon; it's all on the internet.

The soothsayers are alarmed.
Soon the line of tumbrels will start arriving,

there should be little surprise, less resistance.
Then the roundups, each to be put to the test,

the wizened imbeciles already drivelling at the promise
of public burnings and the sight of naked flesh.

Jack Frost

Bankers in their counting houses
 figuring the books,
beauty-parlour lady friends,
 assets are their looks.

Poets in the public houses
 drinking whiskey neat;
Jack Frost clings to their bedposts
 and lives among their sheets.

Manhood

When I read this morning about the locked drawers
and secret cabinets in the museums of the world
where curators store all the penises hacked
in former times from the ancient marble figures

I could not help but imagine those magnificent statues
frozen on their pedestals in timber-floored halls
and cold alcoves, naked,
noble but unmanned,

waiting for the last footfall to echo down
the wide staircases and melt into the evening bustle
before softening out of their poses,
now that the coast is clear,

and slowly contorting,
bending forward at the waist,
stoic white faces scrunched
in agony and humiliation,

curling and cracking onto their hunkers
where they remain, rocking too and fro,
on the balls of perfectly carved feet,
sobbing gently, as they try to come to terms

with their misfortune, innocent of any crime
and baffled by the knowledge that a loin cloth
or even a fig leaf would have saved them
from a world whose rules are no longer on their side.

The Earth Circles the Sun

The day our teacher in a gust of inspiration
called on O'Donnell to stand up at his desk
in the middle of the room –

*Now boys, it's like this,
O Donnell there is the sun,
just look at his big head of red hair.*

We all laughed at lanky O'Donnell
standing up in the middle of the room
and his mad head of red hair.

*You Kelleher, stand over there near the window,
your head is the Earth, what is he boys?*
'The Earth, Sir', we sing-songed.

*Now Gannon, you go over and stand beside Kelleher,
your head is the Moon, what is he boys?*
'The Moon, Sir,' we sing-songed again.

*This is the tricky bit now lads –
Gannon, you start walking in circles around Kelleher.
Kelleher, you start pacing around the room.*

*O'Donnell you stay standing exactly where you are,
and wipe that smirk off your face.
Now, Kelleher, start turning slowly as you go.*

They made their way to the back wall, Kelleher walking
and turning, Gannon circling Kelleher,
then across the room and up the other side.

*Now boys, that's the solar system, the Earth
goes around the Sun, the Moon goes around the earth,
do ye understand?* 'Yes Sir", we chorused.

And how long will it take for Kelleher to get back to the start?
'About three minutes,' Freddy Glynn giddy in the front desk.
You're a fool Glynn, what is he boys? 'A fool, Sir'.

Tell them sun.
'A year Sir, to circle the sun', O'Donnell's face
as red now as his hair.

He praised O'Donnell, explained about leap years,
how given enough space he could set out all the planets
even as far as Pluto.

Then Gannon fell over the rubbish basket,
Kelleher fell over Gannon,
and that ended the lesson.

Kelleher lives today in New York City,
a musician, and a fine one too.
Mike Gannon is in local politics.

Glynn has fingers in many pies
and flies a helicopter, goes racing.
Peter O'Donnell joined the army

and one day on a tour of U.N. duty,
his blue beret tucked under his arm
when he stood up tall on the rampart

to scan the dusty terrain,
a sniper put a bullet in his head.
His red hair an easy target,

even from a mile away,
like the sun, it was said,
against that perfect Lebanese sky.

The Great Empire's Heart

These beggars do not move me,
I see the craft in their outreach,
the stab in the heart of their eyes.

They would melt our bronze statues for washers,
cripple the empire, take warning Gaius,
our shrines and marble gods will be crushed.

I have come to believe the street-rumours,
their villas in the country, stables full of stallions.
Check their toenails for pedicures,

then walk on. Let us not be taken in.
The Forum will not be safe for the likes of us
with our arcades empty, temples forsaken.

I have not always felt like this, but Gaius,
the omens, lightening, and last night a comet. Naivety!
The waters of the bathhouses will freeze.

No, my friend, the beggars do not move me,
the beggars will not move me.

Trap

We lured the troopers out to Hermit's Island
— *the rebels were seen along the shore* —
then slipped the rope and paddled for the mainland;
three weeks they cried for help, then called no more.

Liberation Day

> *Once fully enslaved, no nation, state, city of this earth,*
> *ever afterward resumes its liberty.*
>   – Walt Whitman

When the liberators arrive
the strong will take to the forest,

probably hoping to make it as far as the river –
if there really is a river.

Most will sit about on the caked mud
in that open field some distance from the fence

where rains have been washing bones to the surface.
The air will be filled with the smell of wood-smoke.

TV crews will probably set up satellite dishes near the trees
then the lanes will get wedged with jeeps and lorries.

When light begins to fade most will wander back
and close their own cell doors

to wait for the heavy footsteps in the hallway,
the sound of someone else putting out the lights.

III

There is only one kind of love, but there are a thousand copies, all different.

    from La Rochefoucauld's *Maxims*

By Kingston Bridge

They stood to watch the grey waters
slowdrifting towards the bridge, having come down
from the empty High Street to the river.

Mute-swans stretched their necks but the frail
couple had nothing to offer, no scrap or crust,
so the graceful flotilla paddled away

in the chilly dawn to try their luck
beneath the row of poplars, elegant
and evenly planted along the opposite bank.

Two houseboats lay tight to the gangway,
curtains drawn, one sky blue and freshly painted,
the other, its hardwood cabin pealing,

in need of some attention.
There were bicycles, sturdy, thick-tyred,
clamped together on each deck.

Wouldn't it have been a lovely life, she murmured,
more to herself, perhaps to the river,
but he knew what she meant.

So he took her fragile hand, slightly trembling,
and they turned to find their way
back from where they had come.

The Scene

You know the bar scene where
Miss Hottie arrives into a roomful
of half-drunk, unshaven deadbeats,
wriggling her jailbait cleavage
and tight-jeaned ass to jukebox music.

She chalks a cue then bends over the pool table,
sinking the impossible shot
to stunned silence from the sweaty men,
all strung out on whisky and loneliness,
their wolverine eyes ravishing every sweet inch of her.

The two or three ageing and wasted females
sprawled in corners are not at all pleased.
The tattooed barman, polishing a tumbler,
watches from under heavy eyelids,
waiting for the first hint of rumble.

A beery redneck decides
to make his awkward move
but stumbles into two long-haired weirdo types
and the first punch gets thrown.
Just as Miss Hottie is about to be hauled into a backroom

a figure on a motorcycle drives straight through
the swing doors, spins by the counter,
yells at her to climb aboard
and they're screaming down the highway
before the frozen barroom begins to thaw.

So where do we fit into this scene?
Are you the maiden in distress
or the cool rider to the rescue?
Everybody wants to be the cool rider-to-the rescue,
but who wants to be the redneck or the long-haired weirdo

or the lust-crazed drinker with a week of stubble? Occasionally
someone accepts the role of the giant tattooed barman
but nobody ever wants to be the wasted, ageing female – no,
never the ageing female. Everybody wants to be
Miss Hottie or the motorcyclist.

Just for tonight you can be Miss Hottie
and I will be the cool rider-to-the-rescue.
Tomorrow we will resume our usual roles
but it gets tiresome being the one with the megaphone
always having to call – *Cut*.

Tight Squeeze

What I most remember
about our week together in Paris

is not the pale fresco
we stared at in the Louvre

or the name of the artist
– was he from the Spanish or Flemish School? –

who painted that famous
bowl of shiny fruit.

Even now I can't recall
which King built the splendid pavilions

around the shady garden
where we sheltered one scorching afternoon.

Was it Richelieu or Sully who,
according to the mumbling guide,

lived in the nearby mansion
with the ceilings *remarkably restored*?

I will probably forget the bustling square
with the four Catalpa trees

and the restaurant where we had dinner
three nights in a row

(the handsome waiter having caught your fancy).
Eventually I'll get over the size of the *addition*

for two drinks in that well-known café on a corner,
its name escapes me at the moment.

What I know will remain, however,
is the tight squeeze in the tiny two-person elevator

and those giddy acts of passion snatched
between our fifth floor apartment and ground,

before stepping out like adults
onto the sunny Boulevard

laid out by Baron Haussmann,
the date of which is on the tip of my tongue.

Runaways

Brute equine, tearing strips,
whipped on by the primal,

black holes of separation,
starburst reunions,

not yet the tepid life of polite gestures,
of gazing into the middle distance

like a falconer who knows his favourite
will not be returning from the wild.

Don't Wait

Don't wait for the solder-light
of the November moon,
come to me tonight, my love,

or else I must set out walking
across the broad plain,
through two cities,

the flesh and the bones,
to your estuary,
a living bridegroom.

Everyday, I hear the people
speak of how
they can still see you

coming down for a cup of Jasmine tea
or a bowl of Miso soup.
No, you don't seem far away to me.

Thameslink, Travelling South

Then we are on the move again
crossing Blackfriar's Bridge,
slicing through the wastelands south of the river
roof-high above 'each charter'd street',
post-war brick or 60's brave new worlds,
the silver flash of barbs and spikes,
and litter caught in every weedy trap.

The sudden clatter through a sidewall squeeze,
that even voice naming stations
as if they were all worthwhile.
Further south, houses step away from the tracks,
their backyards mostly no-go zones,
but here and there the optimistic start of lovers,
a shrub perhaps or bright paving slabs,

trellis for a creeper nailed straight up
or pots arranged in clusters, hauled down
from B & Q with dreams of lounging
together in the sun,
their friends around for Sunday afternoon.
Beginnings, middles, endings,
relationships on show in episodes.

But mainly jungle, neglected plots,
more trouble than they're worth.
A fish-pond choked with weeds,
a rusting barbecue used once or twice
and that was that, the weather blamed
or work or health, the way it goes,
resolutions cooling on the lip.

An expensive curve of timber decking
rots behind a house near Streatham.
Laid out some years ago
with the best will in the world,
it's now an empty stage,
the play a flop or pulled
when the star walked from the set.

We pass Lambeth Cemetery, Haydons Road,
and I, with everything on hold,
turn from this dark conjecturing
and the flashing quicksilver beyond the glass
where you stand in every crush and queue,
each aching detail, your hair thrown back,
my body tingling from the certainty of it.

These days I try to come and go like everybody else,
no more straining to see past the immediate.
After all, there is something to be said for a place
that stands, not in anger or even indifference,
with its collar up, its back turned,
a place that leaves you, living still,
but completely and utterly alone.

Only the night before last
as I crossed by the edge of the Common,
a fox came out of the mist through the row of chestnuts,
healthy, well fed, fur damp and flat across his back.
He froze for an instant to measure the hazard,
face and body twisted in that famous curve and grin,
resenting the intrusion, our trivial sharing of a moment.

Mystery

Beyond our bedroom window,
a starry nightsky where light and laws
curve away into mystery

and logic swirls like dust
from a chalkboard
grown wild with equations.

All talk of beginnings
and endings
turns to gibberish

in that state of constant becoming
where the moment
and eternity is one,

embraced, less through reason's
weaving metaphors,
than in the sacred act of love.

Dublin, Early Autumn

Traffic streaming down from Parnell Square,
sunlight pole-dancing on the silver Spire,
prayer groups full belt outside Ann Summer's store,
mysteries of thongs and night attire.
This autumn afternoon, a city stroll,
strange luxury of nothing much to do.
The romance of the bustling Moore Street stalls,
fruits, cut-flowers, but not the place we knew

when years ago, defying the oracle,
we bought your diamond ring not far from here.
In photographs, my god, we are so young.
But now we kiss and know we've come full circle,
same vender's cry – *Flowers for your lady dear?*
Red apples, yes, and white chrysanthemums.

In Cannizaro Park

South London, a working Monday,
nobody about this concealed park,
only a trembling fragility of light and insects,
the musky scent of earth and sap. So silent,
the great metropolis seemed very far way.

I find a suntrapped bench, bleached white
for want of stain. My eyelids heavy
even though my heart is in my mouth.
They would be about it now,
the surgeon and his crew.

Take yourself off to the Common,
the kindly Sister in HDU advised.
We've got your mobile number if needs be.
A city full of strangers,
a sunny September afternoon.

Grey squirrels came to scratch about my bench,
I watched their frenzied capers up and down the trunks,
bushy-tailed, elegant, out along the limbs
like costumed dancers at the Moulin Rouge.
Mischievous yet indifferent, about a business all their own.

When this is all behind us my love,
I will take you here in sunshine to this very bench
and celebrate those cloistered shadows,
that ancient willow, the perfect eucalyptus,
this banquet of colours through the trees.

Time to return. I pass the little pond once again,
the monkish heron stoic in the corner by some reeds.
Now up ahead the hospital, just as I had left it.
Soon there will be news,
with any luck, it will be good.

In the clear skies off to the west
the silver gleam of Boings lining up,
descending into Heathrow one by one,
bellies level and steady, almost miraculous,
everything perfectly under control.

Credo

> *Beauty is truth, truth beauty.*
>   John Keats

Although I believe in nothing now except
the truth of your hand on my bare shoulder
each and every blessed morning

it is more then enough,
more then all the marble floors
and vaulted domes of Christendom.

For sure the time will come when
one of us will wake to loneliness,
its cold breath filling a bedroom,

fumble with buttons, all bearings melted,
no more north and south,
but that shrivelled world is for another time.

Tonight a full and beautiful moon sits
high in its crow's nest
above the tattered rigging of the clouds,

and there are stars, whole galaxies,
the darkness of the universe,
and the darkness beyond the universe.

An Easy Way With Words

Chosen! – I should think not.
More likely, darlin', our existence,
yours, mine, anyone's,
could be put down to a weepy movie,

a heat-wave or a cold snap,
maybe a power cut
or an extra bottle of Chablis
on the way home from the dogs.

No masterplan, my lovely,
no Mr Greybeard's finger,
nothing more special
(and you are special, sugar)

then vague disquiet
on the eve of a notable birthday,
a flight delay, a wet Sunday,
or simply an easy way with words.

Lifers

It's as if they have given up on each other
(were they ever starry-eyed?),
their past crimes far from glamorous,

no jewel heists, no ripping off Las Vegas.
Lifers now, doomed to serve out their time
with bucket and mop,

the brighter one allowed to push the trolley
carrying the cigarettes
and well-thumbed paperbacks,

the wild lovescenes ripped out
and stashed behind secured doors
where they try hard in private

to re-live the favourite moments
from the night of their one Big Bang,
(not that you could call it a big bang)

the memory of which is
best not talked about now,
probably best forgotten.

Dead Windows

Dead windows in a house of mourning,
the walled garden gone wild,
naked fruit trees and brambles up to the door.

Grey rain pawing the bay-window
and the wind in the wide chimney like a child
crying in a locked and empty room.

Circling, Circling

It is the story of a man abroad on the hillside,
heartsore, crying her name, mind in a swirl.

Found days later up there in the ancient ring-fort,
half crazed and famished,

lips chaffed from thirst,
swearing that, try as he might,

circling the stone ramparts
by daylight and moonlight,

the gap below the bulky lintel
refused to show itself,

no toehold could be found
in the high limestone walls.

Folksong for Kitty

I hear your name is Kitty Brosnan,
so they told me in the village,
would you like to be my wife?

Tall wayfarer from the mountain
where they lived on boar and cabbage
promised her a better life.

Built themselves a leaky cabin
in the woods beyond the torrents,
just one room with fire and bed.

Here they fattened up two piglets
she was given by her father,
always went to sleep well fed.

He vanished in the great Black River
trying to snatch the running salmon,
they found his skiff among the reeds.

She raised their only son and daughter,
starless in the hail and storm,
shadowed in her widow's weeds.

Company

Has this been going on for long?
We'll need to set an extra place,

a knife and fork, a glass and jug.
Those gestures to some imaginary third,

a side glance at that empty chair.
There you go again, left eyebrow

raised to invisible camera three.
Some creature with a claw and beak

is up and prowling in your cage.
I'll let things sit for now and eat

but soon I think we'll have
that talk….alone.

Blink

Cold floor
a cat
wooden building blocks
then school
you cry
exams
you slam some doors
buy a rusting crock
girls' lovely thighs
I do
a kid
then three
the job goes well
a house
with grass
hobbies
a week or two abroad
your daughter falls in love
a son implodes
grandchildren hug your neck
a cat
plastic building blocks
a doctor shakes his head
you…

Country Matters

It was all about boundaries,
rights of way,
the walled orchard,
the hedged meadow
with passage to water,
stile, gate or garden path.

Knowing the steps,
the waltz of it and strands
of tangled generations
traced by old men and old women,
mindful of difficult calvings,
judging the distance between two hip bones.

Eyes of Blue

A lifetime later,
her waltz-by-a-river eyes

are now frost-frozen
in her head,

like the two vagrants,
found battered and dumped

on the waste ground
near the river.

They might have survived
the paper said, only for the snow.

Cultural Evening

(A non-literary ballad)

I'm squarin' up to have a go at Mattie Burke
from back the West, when Mattie's mate
'Geronimo' Mc Mahon tears off shirt
and vest then swings a pool-ball
in a sock, I hear the whoosh
fly past my ear, duck and jab him
in the rocks, he's down
an gawkin' lakes of beer.

I hate to see fine drink wasted,
Big Rita, alone at the bar, gulps down
Mc Mahon's Crested Ten – it's true,
Big Rita loves her jar. Burke, I think,
dodged out the back; 'Geronimo'
hunched as in a womb, Big Rita
winks, says – *You're some crack,*
I think it's time to take me home.

Gothic

All the dark night
gales raced through the hill country
and a storm rumbled over the village.

Streams spilled down the tangled lanes
and the rotting ash tree tumbled,
blocking the east bridge.

At daybreak they found a headstone uprooted
in the old churchyard, felled
by the winds or lightening maybe.

Some called it coincidence
but was it not a year to the very day
since the young Squire remarried?

Now his first wife's gravestone
lay shattered amid whispers of haste,
unseemly haste.

Homecoming

Even with a clogged burner in the kitchen stove
and the strange smell oozing from somewhere
beneath the sink, it is comforting to know
that one can risk walking naked from the shower
all the way to the wardrobe without someone
from housekeeping appearing
to ask if the bed needs turning down.

So let us celebrate our homecoming
with a bottle of the worst possible plonk
selected, without care or attention,
from our infamous 'bad-year cellar'
housed on top of the clogged washing machine,

leaving it to breathe while we visit the village
in a car with deflated tyres, to buy crackers
and cheese from the first person in weeks
able to call us by our own unfamiliar
yet legally-held names.

And let there be no pang of conscience
for not making an effort to return
via the scenic route, with the aid
of a crumpled map, because one is comforted to know

that in this neck of the woods there stands
nothing more impressive
than the well stocked if shambolic yard
of 'The Handy Hardware Store'
boldly serving its customers 'Since 1965'.

Making Plans

We could always strike out for the mountains above
or wander the dusty villages
but it's bumper-to-bumper out there
and the price of juice.

The dirt-track is filling up with tourists in jeeps,
where are they all going in this heat?
Anyway, it's been done, it's all been done,
so let's just stay here, you and I,

open the blue port-hole in the gable,
there is nobody listening, nothing drooling
in the tall grass, only the cicadas and
the red breeze. Lie, lie, hear the carillon…

Tonight, long-dead stars will be pumping overhead
and you can be naked, so can I.
This is an island after all,
we're not fully in control.

Now That You Are Gone

Morning songbirds
in the trees about the house,

and not a single note between them
in their featherheads.

Downstairs, the polite silence of the livingroom,
the cushions you bought in Dublin,

the drapes you stitched and lined last Christmas.
Yes, all of that, and my stubbled heart,

the one you said I liked to keep in solitary,
growing fonder, fonder, fonder.

The Reading

> *Everything is going to be all right.*
>   from a poem of the same name by Derek Mahon.

A grey Galway evening threatening rain,
the stony hills of Clare astray in the mists,
the big window, the garden, then the sea.

A shaft of pale sunlight breaks through across the bay
as if to finger the resting place of some forgotten hermit
or a nook where long-dead lovers dreamed and kissed.

Soon the sky closes again like a heavy book
and drizzle thickens once more
all the way to the end of the Pier.

I hear the 'beep, beep' of your text.
It is later then I think, shadows and silence
and the house growing cold.

My awkward thumb replies – *Sleep tight all fine xx*.
I find the poem by Derek Mahon
and read it aloud to the empty room

and for you in that distant city, over the worst.
Yes, his words are true and comforting.
It *is going to be all right*.

IV

Ah, yes, I wrote 'The 'Purple Cow' –
I'm sorry now I wrote it.
But I will tell you, anyhow,
I'll kill you if you quote it!

GELETT BURGESS

Winner

Claims he's happier now with a proper job,
corner window, a desk, good commission.
No longer scribbling lines into dog-eared notebooks,
he's a winner, making big decisions.

Gone the fear of bills and slips saying rejection.
No grey areas. People ask him things.
Money, nice house – 'Xanadu', a woman's affection,
colleagues who come at weekends for dinner.

Twice a year he visits the city,
bitter in The Wellington, Arsenal at home.
There's a number he calls. She comes straight over.
Just read, he whispers, *read softly to me,*
of the 'caves of ice', the 'pleasure dome',
and later we can sing 'of Mount Abora'.

Creatures of the Mist

I come upon the tracks of deers' hooves in the snow.
Language but no words.
      Tomas Transtromer, from *March 1979*,
      translated by Robin Fulton.

Grey shadows emerging
out of the mists,
drawing closer, gesturing
that they are famished.

One or two, I can see, are
wrapped like mummies,
horror figures,
no eyes, no ears.

How many are out there?
A shuffling army?
Drawn to me as if
words could help their deformities,

nourish them in their terrible silence
or give them shelter,
but they are not creatures of shelter
they are creatures of the mists.

Bloodless ethereals,
do they want my blood? Let them
perish! Perhaps they have already perished.
What do you want of me?

My cry fades and there is nothing to be done,
at least for now,
nothing, except record their passing,
record that they at least exist.

Fatal Distractions

I think I will become a monk
with bell and cell and little bunk,

live a life of contemplation
walled away from all temptation,

spend my days with ink and quill,
never have to pay a bill,

reject the flesh, the pub at night –
and then, perhaps, I'll start to write.

Meet the Punctuations

At least with Full Stop
you know where you stand,
ole' door slammer,
time-bell chimer,
protector of virgins,
back-of-the-shovel tapper
to the full-bellied grave.

Don't let him get a liking for you
and watch for his schizophrenic
half-brother Semi-Colon;
that nod-and-wink weathercock,
whatever-you're-having-yourself merchant,
Mr Wishy-Washy
neither here nor there

and his side-kick
Apostrophe,
who comes out to play
when the Vowels are off resting,
he's the opportunist of the flock,
first sub' on the local team,
can get a little possessive.

Then there's Flash Harry himself
The Dash –
back from Amherst,
all arty airs and breathless – indecision,
out of work a lot these days,
typecast or so he says
after that big thing with Emily.

You could only pity poor stick-in-the-mud
Colon putting up with them all,
keeping sentry at the gate,
with his clipboard, ticking the list,
the quartermaster of the family
left holding the fort when Dash
took off for the New World.

Dependable though, he will keep order:
unlike the real playboy of the family
the volatile E mark!
The sunbathing stud,
the most erotic of the Punctuations.
Look at him standing there,
proud, erect, stiff as a poker.

Cast your eyes over simple words
like Ouch! Yes! Oh! and even Ah!
See how they react in his sleazy company.
In fact, no word is safe from
Mr Ever Ready. Use me, he insists,
use me often, especially at weekends
when the neighbours are away!

Ode to a Rejected Cliché

Behold our old Cliché asleep in the gutter,
once spoken of proudly, now reduced to a mutter,
the envy of all but soon over-exposed,
an unwanted lover, neglected, ignored.

Famed for your charm, you survive on past glories,
confined to sports pages and foul tabloid stories.
For services rendered you got little thanks,
all authors are fickle, all critics are cranks.

Who could forget the whoops of delight
when The Poet embraced you that very first night?
But writers are ruthless when it comes to their page,
you tried to return, they reacted with rage.

So our Cliché's career slid into decline,
from the famed Poet's verse sunk to ballads and rhyme,
down to pop-songs, live football and late-night T.V.,
into taxi-men's chatter, then the pubs on the quay.

If you're now disregard, prey tell, where's the sin?
You will probably find Jesus and become born again,
pick up with a preacher then all will be fine,
for the shelf-life is longer in the religious line.

Sensing the Verse

Listen with your eyes wide open,
and watch with your ears pinned back.

Feel the pulse
with the tips of your fingers trembling.

Stalk the kaleidoscope of words
as they bleed towards the core

to the great pumping heart full of blood.
Careful, take great care,

here the ground can swallow,
here you will be astray.

From such a place, no one has ever returned untouched
and for this you may not always give thanks.

The Way With Strangers

He was living – no, he was spending time,
behind a lattice window on the upper floor
of a very narrow townhouse with a death-trap
balcony, green wrought iron, last lick of paint
applied sometime between wars.

There was a table in the corner
with a scatter of books, writing materials,
an array of pared pencils
and large sheets of white paper,
everything he thought he would need
ready and waiting.

It was a solid four-square wooden table,
dependable, with a chair to match.
He would sit there for hours,
muttering oaths and gurgling to himself.

> *Things, everything, has ground to a halt.*

Mornings were the worst. Not mornings exactly,
more that moment when sleep let him slip from its fog
like a great bird emerging above a place
where those terrible conspiracies devised on Olympus
have at last been played out.

Someone, maybe the original owners,
had installed a block-and-tackle pulley
out on the trembling balcony,
but with nothing to pull and nothing to tackle
for decades, it had seized, become an artefact.

> *Face it, the plan has come unstuck.*

The room was small with a sloping ceiling,
worn floorboards and faded, pale-green wallpaper.
From the window, looking left,
he could see the fountain or most of it,
and the little square where locals and a few strangers
gathered in the evenings at its two dingy cafes.

Here the drinkers watched each other
through falling spouts of water,
wondering if life was any better
for those on the opposite side.

> *In my sleep I often mistake that bubbling water*
> *for the music of home.*

The locals greeted him now on sight, a smile, a wave,
but always that second look, surreptitious.
They thought he was a writer.
A waitress once asked if he were a poet.
It made sense at the time to say he was.
She smiled, he laughed – they took it from there.

> *They will all smile until I can no longer pay,*
> *such is the way with strangers.*

His view was across the Old City, terracotta rooftops,
slanting, some sagging as if exhausted by the strain.
A warren of narrow alleys surrounded their little quarter.
Morning sunlight could touch the doorways near the square
washing them clean of the night's woes.

Late one evening a drunken couple tried to make love
in the shadows beneath his window.
They had been seen drinking all afternoon
around the fountain but it was not to be their night.
They both grew impatient
then angry at the failure.
Things did not end well.

> *Brute force does not work. Being obstinate*
> *is neither easy nor fair. Surrender should*
> *not always be a last resort.*

As autumn wore on
and he had nothing to show for his time,
the people in the cafes began to question him.

They told him that in winter a cold wind
comes knifing off the river
and the people who have to stay in these alleys
become sharp and unpleasant.
He said he was used to the cold.

Then they asked if he would be leaving.
At the time he was not sure where else he could go.

Trespasser

Thoughts enter through the green zone
loud but hauling empty baggage,
nothing at all to declare.

I have become a stranger,
an impostor
trespassing in my own head.

My daily walk to the shore
is now only a hunt for a good place
to scatter ashes.

At night I lie awake listening
to the edge of my world
crumbling and flaking away.

V

Till then I see what's really always there:
Unresting death, a whole day nearer now,…

PHILIP LARKIN

Old Vixen

Little more then skin and bone,
full length beneath the green blanket-brambles,
no slink now, no bound,
her once keen whiff grown ropey.

She knows. She knows that soon
her carcass will stiffen
for magpie and rook,
soft eyes pecked from her skull.

It is time, her long jaw stretches out,
time to let that dark terror
skulking on the fringe of her senses
close in, it has her measure at last.

Mother Fox, Mother Fox,
who can save you now?

The Lie

I watched you in the rear-view mirror
hunched by the door,

clutching the brown leather travel bag,
the one you bought for that last trip to Lourdes.

The letter for the nursing home
pulsed like a detonator in my breast pocket.

It was a sunny afternoon, mid February,
fresh buds and splashes of early daffodils.

Just 'till you get on your feet,
a week or two at most.

Your sharp eyes pinned me to the seat,
the shaft of the lie twisting in my chest.

November

of the rook's black eye,
the magpie's deranged cackle,

a widow's mantilla stretched
across the face of the moon.

Nightwatch

The sun came up red and gold
from behind the trees
filling your room with comfort.

In ones and twos the good people slipped away
having kept the nightwatch, the small hours
thwarted, at least for the time being.

Sleeping, breathing, sleeping,
as we read each eyelid's sparrow-flicker
for a sign of waking. But you were beyond sleep,

drifting out past sight of land
on an ebbing tide,
you would not be coming back.

Then, for a short while,
just the two of us,
were we ever closer?

As I chattered, your lip curled,
our last connection,
I hold it was a smile.

Daytime bustle along the corridor;
the kindly Doctor's hand on my shoulder,
I think she is nearing the end.

The world snagged its axis,
shuddered,
spun on.

A February Burial

The air crisp as fresh bedlinen,
a February sun drawing the chill
from the old gravestones,
the earth wakening again
and hungry for what it needs.

Someone has draped a rug of plastic grass
across the mound of freshly-dug clay,
as if clay was embarrassing, out-of-place,
not a full participant,
like a drunk uncle out cold at a wedding.

Cars pass by and a double-decker bus.
Those upstairs allow themselves a glance
and then away about their business,
a little unsettled but not for long

because the day-to-day has already told them
it will never come to this.
No way, it whispers, at least for you,
could it ever come to this.

The Day After

The dawn symphony begins
in the trees around our house
and I am grateful for your warm hand
in mine, no need for anything more.

It is hard to pin things down
the wrecking-ball still spinning.
I have no answers, no questions;
her last sigh, a moth in a vast cathedral.

There is backfilling to be done,
aftershocks, resettling,
then the tools must be washed
and stored carefully away.

At Grattan Road

The tide is out at Grattan Road today.
The wrinkled sand lying bare and grey as skin
one glimpses in long-wards where old women
discard their quilts and call you close to say
they know your face but then a vacant stare.
A mist is building, yet the light streams through
here and there along the causeway to
the island and in beams across to Clare.

That photograph, same spot but years ago,
Mother, her sister, daughters, only son.
Two smiling women, summer frocks. One gone,
the other in a London nursing home.
From up the shore the pungency of rot,
a lobster-boat from Claddagh hauling pots.

The Door

> *At the end of suffering*
> *there was a door.*
>   from The Wild Iris by Louise Glück

Even though I knew you would bring ease,
I had been dreading the rattle
of your black chariot, the snarling
and straining of your sleek-skinned dogs.

In the end you came alone by the back roads,
took the moss-covered avenue, gentle as a herdsman,
no clang, no clamour, only the colours
draining from the bed of wild bluebells,

and the rooks high on the ash-boughs
falling silent as you passed.
Then your shadow at the side door
and the sun dipping behind O'Malley's Wood.

Barbs

The barbs are in the minor things,
the pop-ups, the out-of-the-blues,
a spoon rattling in a china teacup.

Dreams, strange worlds, your voice
in snatches, a verse, the wind –
hard to pin it all down,

the earth neither flat nor round
yet everyone very kind,
handshakes and *sorry for your troubles*.

Too late now, far too late,
for all those *should have dones*
and *could have dones*

whispering through your half-sleep,
like faint pleadings from behind
the high graveyard wall.

Beggars

There must be room for mourning too
in this sparkling city
of courteous arrogance.

Those shiny towers promising immortality
– keep them, keep it all –
it's only a trembling valley of bolted doors.

I make for the hills in a speed-blur,
ambers, reds, electric blues.
From up here I can see more clearly,

temples, theatres, houses of learning and lies.
And overhead? The silent insolence of the stars.
We are less then beggars. In the end

we could not steal or borrow one extra hour for you,
with all our great powers, not even a last,
beautiful, twinkling second.

Birthday Drive

I

The empty road runs west through miles of pine,
a great lake always off to the right, hidden

behind trees or a ridge but the flaky hoardings
– Boats-for-Hire, Fishing Lodge – say it's there.

Every place closed and shuttered, out of season.
Geese pass overhead, instinct stretching out in a V.

And then the lake's grey waters swing into view,
and all those lonely islands,

one, as the locals will tell you,
for every wet day of the year.

II

The day began with thin Spring sunlight
shape-shifting across the silver mountains,

ambers and browns rising out on the bogs.
I passed the dark lake where thirty years ago

they dumped that poor girl's body
after holding her a week in the woods.

A dingy craft-shop, wrong time of year, no postcard,
no scone, no slice of wholemeal bread.

How you loved to fill the house
with the hungry scent of fresh baking.

I took the Sky Road, parked near a tufty field, stared
across the great ocean crawling below.

They captured the rebels out there on Omey Island,
hanged them all at Ballynahinch.

III

Dear Mother,

It is March nineteenth.
I am writing this note to go with your birthday card,
the one I did not buy,
(no cards in this craftshop, only weak tea)
the one that will not be delivered
because it is more than a year now
since we kept the nightwatch.
Could you hear the people at your bedside,
old friends, family, the good folk who cared?
I felt you would not leave
until there was only ourselves,
and I was right.
Not knowing what to do then,
the rituals I mean,
I whispered nothing into your ear,
no gesture of tenderness,
it was not our way.
But I opened the window,
just a little behind the curtain,
I don't know why,
some atavistic urge.

Building a home in the land of the dead
had been your life for years,
even before the cancer bit,
this world had not been kind.

We followed your funeral instructions to the letter,
the clothes you wished to wear,
the simple music, the few special prayers.
I never told you
how much I admired your courage –
(we did not speak so directly,
the symbolic being easier somehow)
as you battled every step of the way,
stubborn and infuriatingly independent.
When I asked if you would give up the chemo'
I was dismissed as a quitter.
In the early days, I often called
to bring you home from treatment
only to find you had taken the bus.

There are many things I want to say on your birthday
but I'm not sure what…
it's too elusive,
like catching trout with bare hands
or counting stars.
Instead, I came out here to the mountains.
Tomorrow I will bring you daffodils
cut from your own garden,
I will stand by your resting place
and try to believe…
that you have at last found ease,
that in some way you are happy,
if only in dreamless sleep,
if only in black oblivion.

Your loving son.

Intruder

I open the door with a freezing cold key.
Your house swings around to the north,

hunches its gabled shoulders,
the coats on the hall-stand turn their backs.

The fern by the telephone is browning
and drooping with thirst.

Everything else just as you left it,
six-week old newspaper, white walking-shoes

under the chair. I bundle the letters,
check all the windows, sit for a while

in the lifeless kitchen,
no rattle from the cutlery drawer,

no gurgle and click from your kittle,
no reply from the bedroom down the hall.

And yet I answer the silence: *Only me,
just passing, don't bother with tea.*

Sorrow

When I wake, the trembling light
is aquarium blue
and I am flatnosed
against curved glass,
like a tourist in a windowed submarine,
watching the easy flag-wave
of a great fishtail pass by.

I can taste salt, feel the swelling fathoms.
This is ocean, dangerous, unpredictable.
The slow bend of another big fish circling,
blue and blubbery and something even bigger
stirring in its hidey-hole
deep beneath the silt,
layers and layers of it.

Alone

It comes at night when she is alone,
through the bald winter fields,
to skulk around her house
or stand watching from the shadows,

its dark bulk glimpsed
in the turning of the gable,
a stench, like rotting seaweed,
seeping in at the door.

It comes because she is alone,
face stained, wide awake
in their bed – only her bed now,
learning the new language of grief.

It comes when she is standing
at her kitchen sink, evening
tight against the pane, washing
one cup, one plate, one knife, one fork, one spoon.

No Gardener

He gets down as often as he can,
trims and touches up the place,

but he is not handy, no gardener, not like his father,
stays a night or two then off again.

She says she is coping on her own,
night-dreads are never mentioned.

Anyway, the evenings are starting to stretch,
there's a little growth, the world spinning on.

Soon the cherry-blossoms will appear.
Last year the petals stayed a month or more,

no April winds, calm well into May,
nothing, she thought, to trouble them at all,

no hint of brewing storms,
no sign of rain.

Rituals: A Diptych

Keened, he will be washed and readied
by the three women, neighbours will settle
him tidy in the frilled box, beads and scapular,
wisps of grey hair combed back from his forehead.

'Watched' through two full nights, his last
hours before the clay. No shortcuts can be taken,
shouldered in turns from one side of the village to the
other, then across the bridge, for water settles the spirit.

Stones will be carried to be heaped at the halfway mark,
white horses kept away. A stranger happening by
must follow along. Thrice around the crossed spades,
then down easy to face the morning sun.

    ★   ★   ★

Traffic backed up on both sides, the village clogged
and grumbling. Lights green but no go.

Trucks fuming in their own diesel-haze;
resigned drivers listening to the phone-ins.

Something should be done about it!
Up in the new cemetery a mechanical digger

stands a little way off, its steel arm bent to a
resting claw, like a long-necked grazing beast.

The paunchy driver sits in the little cab,
checks his watch again, eyes the gathering,

itching to backfill, to be away, just as soon as the last
straggling mourner turns for the gate.

Solace

Freefalling in the small hours,
your vital signs tubed but fading

and I useless by your bedside,
without the ripcord of prayer,

the comfort of ritual, sacred relic
or water from a holy well. Not even

the solace of all the blessed candles
lit by your thoughtful friends.

No plea-bargaining
with a favourite saint,

rejecting even the temptation
to cry out to the spirit of a dead parent

for a sign that you might pull through,
or at the very least, get one last chance

to take a single silver breath unaided,
then leave of your own wild will.

Wake Talk

There are no pockets in a shroud,
no doors in a tombstone.
   True for you, no truer word.

And you won't find a tow-bar on a hearse.
   A fact, a fact!

Lots of fine people under stones
above in Rahoon Cemetery tonight.
   True for you, that's true for sure.

They'd give their jawbone to be here
with us supping their little drop.
   A fact, a fact!

And another good man joining them
up there tomorrow.
   True for you, marked absent tonight!

One more stroked off our roll.
   The same again Jack, like a good man.

Well said, well said. We'll be long enough dry.
   A fact, a fact!

Seeker's Lullaby

No sign
   no sign at all
not in the tipping sky
   puffy puffy
look in the shelter
down by the black rocks
   splashy splashy
no sign there
nor along the shore
brown weed rotting
and the sandflies
   hoppy hoppy
all the way to the village
the baker
his dog in the backyard
not there not there
across to the butcher
   choppy choppy
mince and pudding
to the café surely in the café
   empty empty
chess-board floor
knight pawn king queen
climb the hill
   climbing climbing
see all about seek all around
no sign
   no sign at all
headstones warming in the sun
the warm sun
   shining shining
growing tired growing sleepy
lie down rest lie down
here

let the grass grow over
    growing growing
little roots
earth tendrils
toe holds
    crawling crawling
no sign
no sign at all
in the rain softening
the wind riotous
the flake melting
the bolt angry
the clouds darkening
    rumble rumble
the grass growing over
no sign
nothing
sleep now
the clay softening
only sleep
nothing else
nothing
nothing at all.

About the Author

At Grattan Road is Gerard Hanberry's third collection of poetry, following *Rough Night* (2002) and *Something Like Lovers* (2005), both from Stonebridge Publications, Wales. 'Poetry on the Dart' (Dublin's version of 'Poems on the Underground') featured a poem during the summer of 2007. In 2004 he was awarded the Brendan Kennelly/ Sunday Tribune Poetry Prize. Gerard holds an MA in Writing from the National University of Ireland, Galway where he teaches a creative writing seminar to undergraduates and delivers the poetry module on the Evening BA Degree course. He also teaches English at his own 'alma mater', St Enda's College, Salthill. Gerard is a member of the advisory panel to the Cúirt International Festival of Literature. He lives with his wife Kerry in their home on the edge of Galway Bay where they raised their family of four, three sons, Jamie, Daniel and Greg and their daughter Jane.